TECHNOLOGY AND INVENTIONS FROM ANCIENT EGYPT THAT SHAPED THE WORLD

HISTORY FOR CHILDREN CHILDREN'S ANCIENT HISTORY

Speedy Publishing LLC
40 E. Main St. #1156
Newark, DE 19711
www.speedypublishing.com
Copyright 2017

In this book, we're going to talk about technology and inventions from Ancient Egypt. So, let's get right to it!

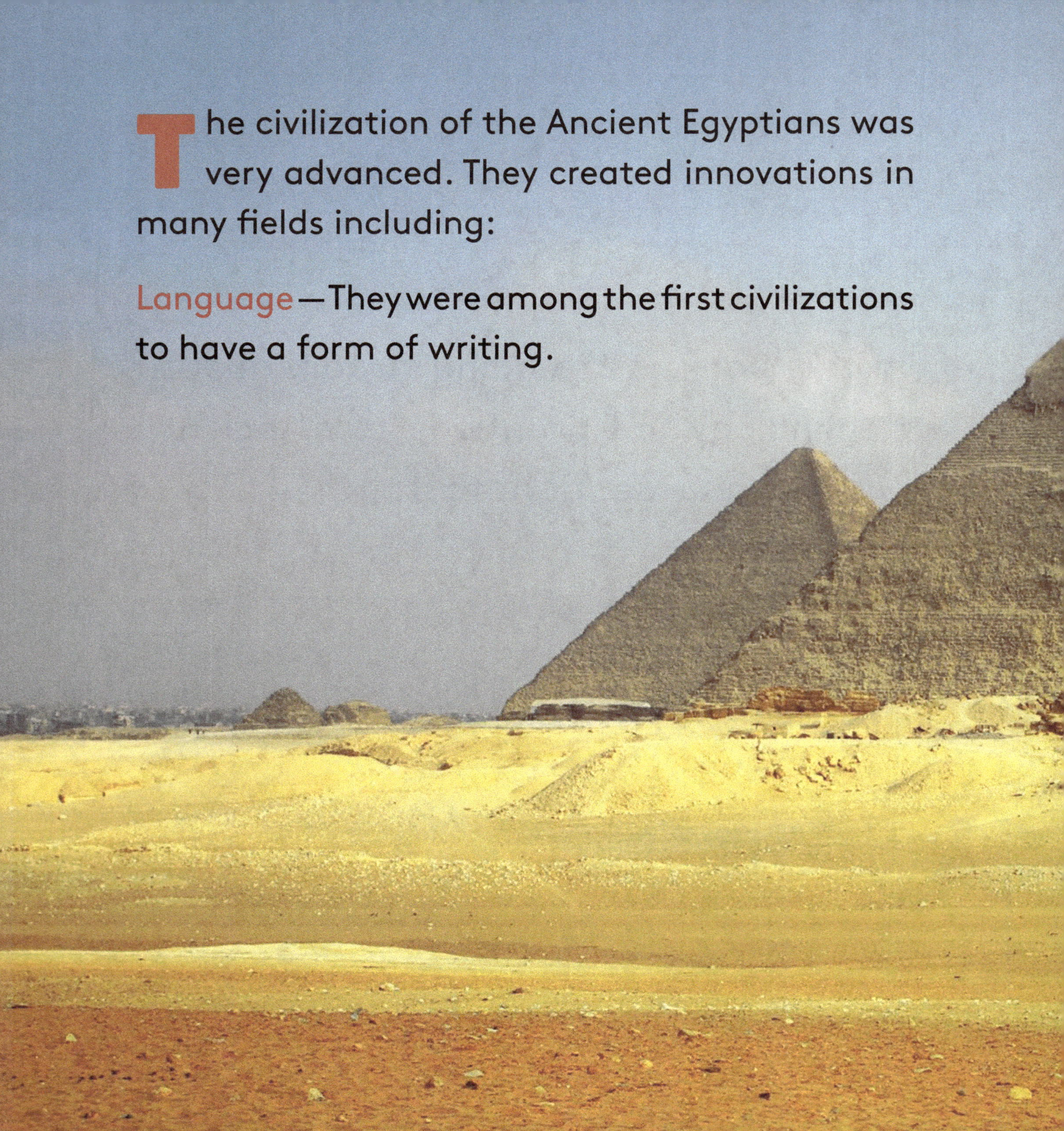

The civilization of the Ancient Egyptians was very advanced. They created innovations in many fields including:

Language—They were among the first civilizations to have a form of writing.

Architecture — They built immense temples and pyramids, which would be difficult to build today.

Astronomy — They used their knowledge of the night sky to create a lunar calendar.

HIEROGLYPHICS

The Egyptians invented one of the earliest forms of writing called hieroglyphics. It was a complex combination of writing using pictures that told stories and symbols that used phonetic sounds. Despite the complexity of their writing, the Egyptians wrote a great deal about the events in their history.

They also used writing to keep accurate records and to document their beliefs. Their hieroglyphic writing appears on some of the most ancient artifacts in the world today. It took many years for scholars to translate hieroglyphics, but there are now Egyptologists who can read and interpret these ancient writings. Thanks to these ancient documents we know a lot about their history and culture.

PAPYRUS OF ANI

PAPYRUS

The Ancient Egyptians learned how to farm the papyrus plant, which grew naturally near the Nile River. With this plant, they created the first sheets of papyrus, a type of durable paper.

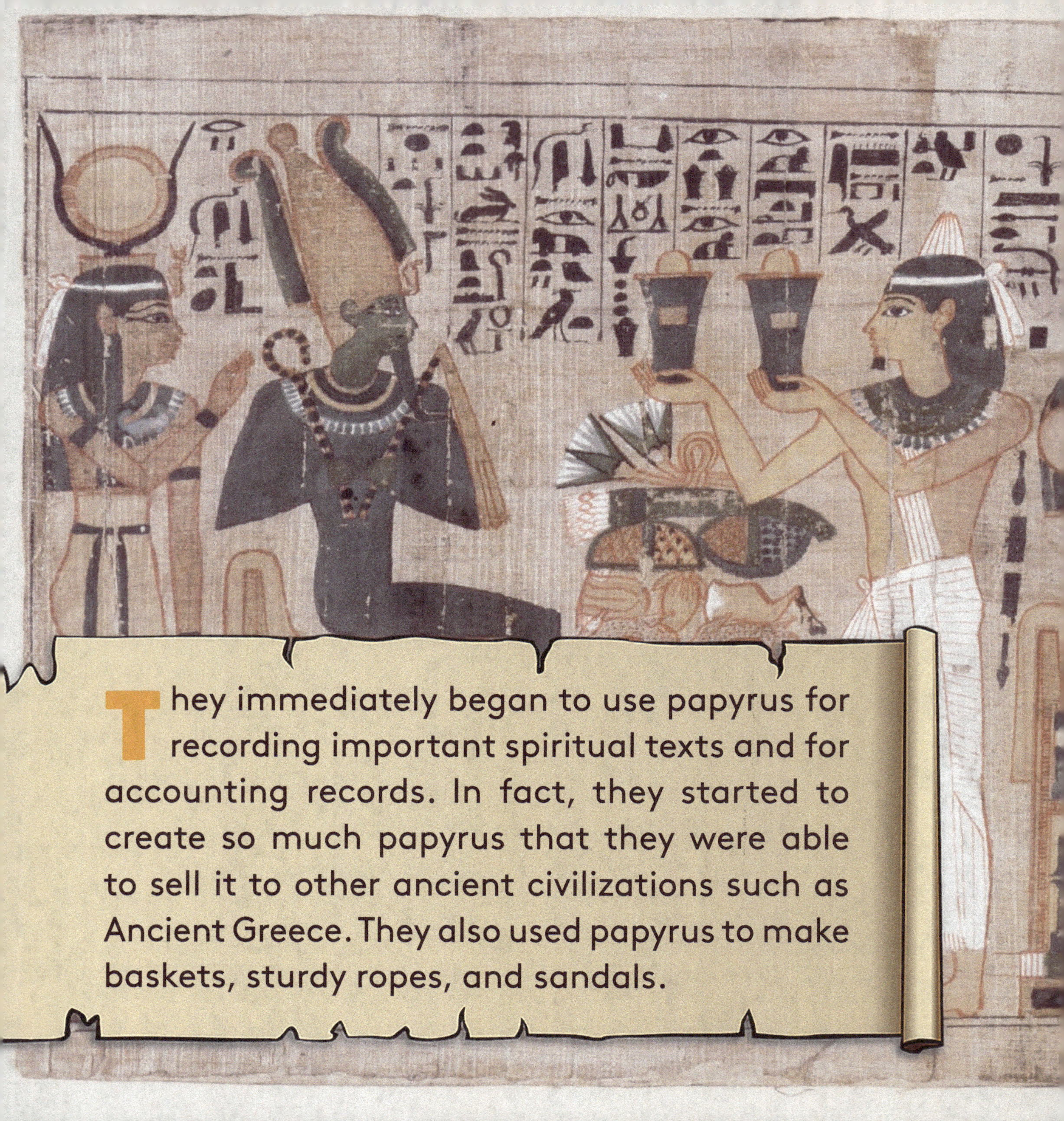

They immediately began to use papyrus for recording important spiritual texts and for accounting records. In fact, they started to create so much papyrus that they were able to sell it to other ancient civilizations such as Ancient Greece. They also used papyrus to make baskets, sturdy ropes, and sandals.

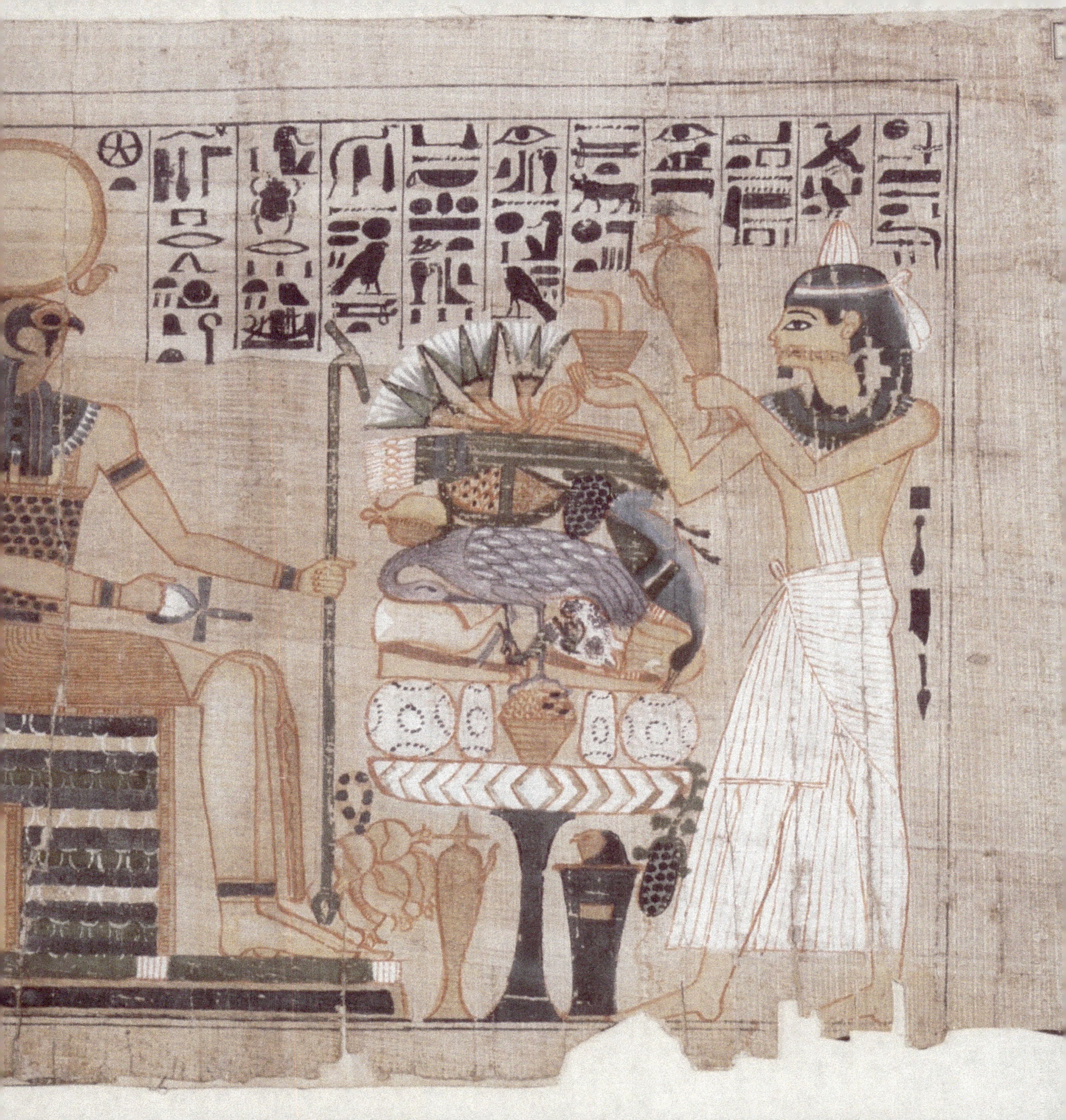

Ancient Ink

INK

Now that they had papyrus they could write on, the Egyptians needed something they could use to write with. They invented black ink and red ink from naturally available sources such as soot and charcoal for black and iron oxide for red.

They used thin reeds as their "pens." They also created the first artificial colors of blue, green, and yellow from different chemical compounds. The Egyptians were masterful with inks and dyes and many of the wall paintings and manuscripts they created have brilliant colors even after thousands of years.

Ancient Pens

EGYPTIAN CALENDAR

CALENDARS

The Egyptians were using a type of calendar they developed over 5,000 years ago. They watched the cycle of the moon and created their calendar on this cycle. Their calendar had 12 months. They organized the different months into three seasons instead of the four we recognize today. Their seasons matched with the increasing and decreasing waters of the Nile River.

They soon discovered that their calendar wasn't as accurate as they wished. The Nile River flooded at the end of June, but it didn't flood right on schedule. Sometimes it was a week later and sometimes it was ten weeks later.

In an effort to make their calendar more accurate so they could predict the flooding, they watched the bright star Sirius and its position relative to the Sun. Then they applied those astronomy principles to create a much more accurate calendar. We still use their model today.

CLOCKS

The Ancient Egyptians were one of the first civilizations to come up with devices that were designed to keep time. The passing of time during the day was determined by the sun's position and the shadows it cast. The passing of time during the night was determined by the positions of the stars.

T hey created:

- **Sundials** and shadow clocks, which used a stationary arm that would cast a shadow when hit by the sun onto a plate divided out by the hours in a day

- **Merkhets**, which used a bar with a plumb line that was attached to a wooden handle to track the alignment of stars to tell the time at night

Sundial

Obelisks, which were monuments that served many purposes and that also cast shadows used for telling time

Water clocks, which were bowl-shaped and had a hole in the bottom so water could rise within the bowl in a regulated way and the water line would represent the time

The **water clocks** were designed for the temple priests because they needed accurate measurements of time that were independent of the sun. They were indoors in the temple and needed to know the time so they could conduct ceremonies on schedule.

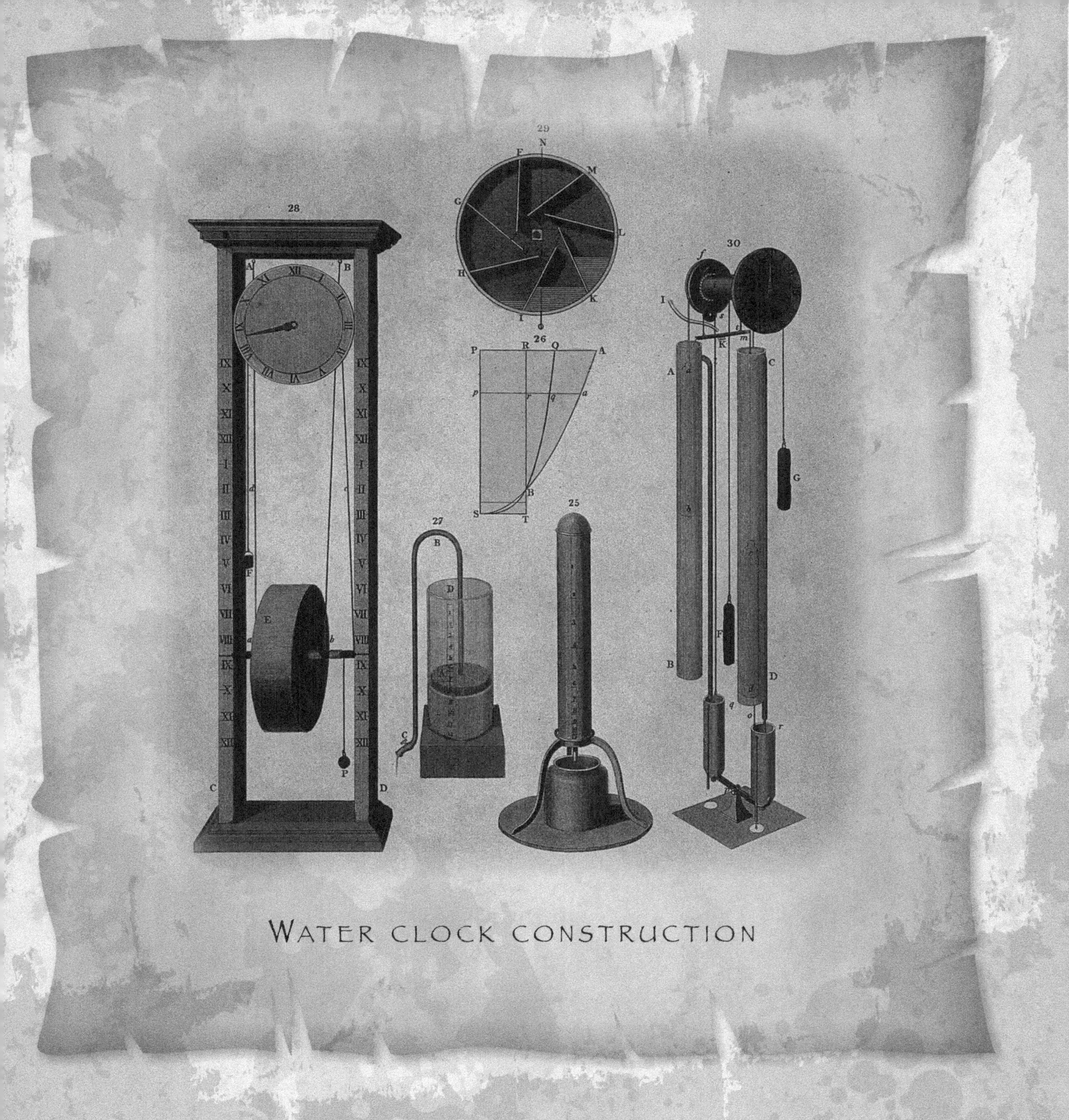

WATER CLOCK CONSTRUCTION

Pyramids

ARCHITECTURE AND CONSTRUCTION

The Ancient Egyptians are known for their amazing architectural designs and feats of construction. It took some time for them to develop the appropriate design for the pyramid, but the pyramids that are standing today, like the Great Pyramid at Giza, are some of the construction marvels of the ancient world.

They also built enormous temples with huge sculptures, many of which are still standing today.

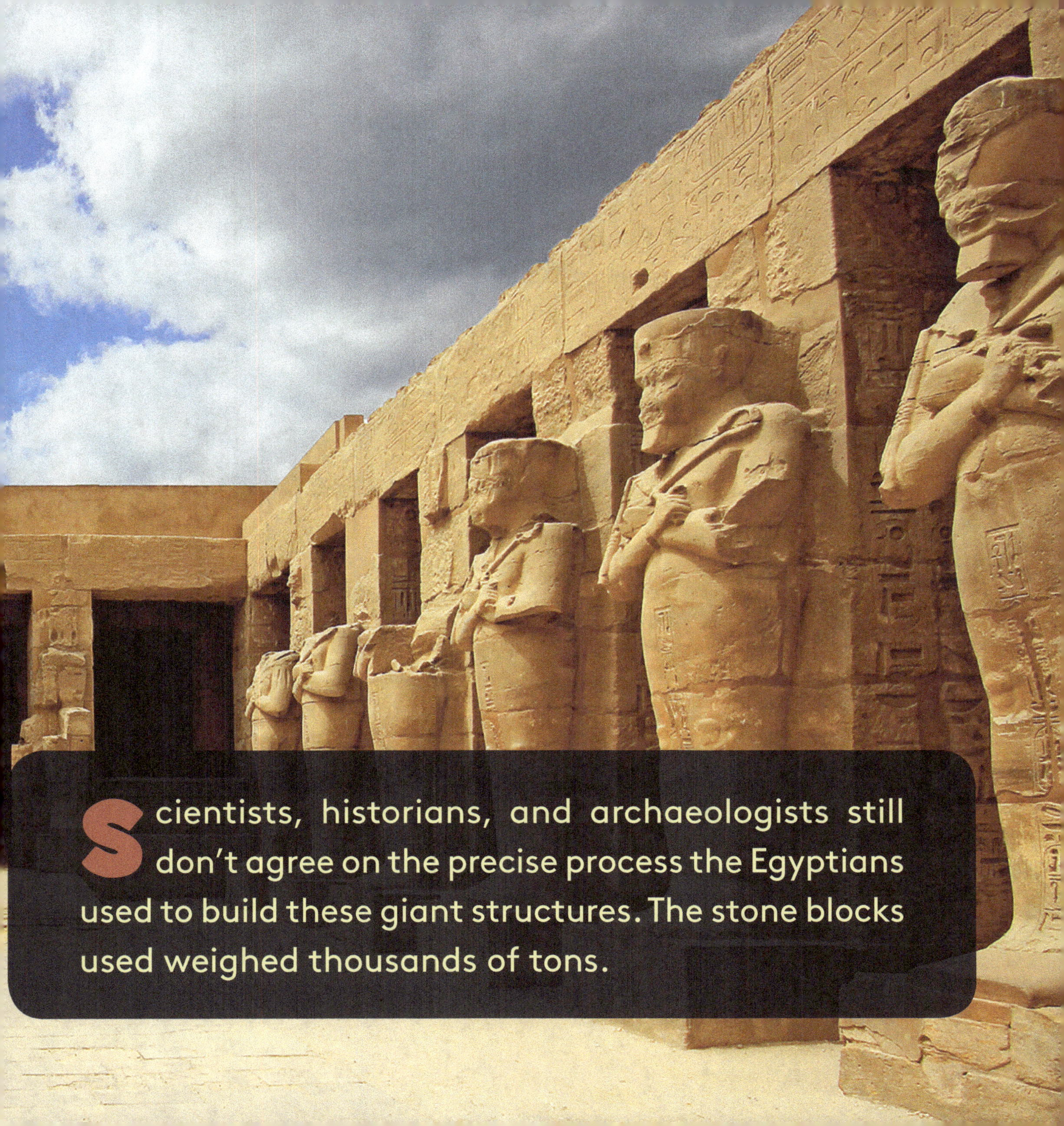

Scientists, historians, and archaeologists still don't agree on the precise process the Egyptians used to build these giant structures. The stone blocks used weighed thousands of tons.

WORKERS TRANSPORTING STONE BLOCK

ORGANIZED LABOR

Not only did the Egyptians create, design, and build these massive structures, they also created the first group of organized laborers. The management of such a huge labor force over decades took a huge amount of skill, communication, and organization. It's been estimated that it took 25,000 to 100,000 workers to build Giza's Great Pyramid.

SIMPLE MACHINES

To help them in the construction of the pyramids and other buildings, the Egyptians created simple machines. They invented ramps and levers to move stones from place to place and to position them. We still use these simple machines in construction work today.

ANCIENT EGYPTIANS BUILDING A PYRAMID

EGYPTIAN BOAT

SHIPS AND NAVIGATION

The Nile River was a perfect waterway for transportation and the Ancient Egyptians soon learned to build small boats made of papyrus reeds. They graduated to building larger ships made of cedar wood.

In addition to these innovative constructions, they learned to use the principles of aerodynamics to make their vessels streamlined. They built rope trusses to make the ship's beams stronger and were the first people to attach rudders mounted on the sterns of their ships.

ANCIENT EGYPTIAN FARMER

AGRICULTURE

Farming was vitally important to the Egyptians. They fed their own people and had crops leftover to sell. They developed the first ox-drawn plows to help them till the soil. This type of plow was used as early as 2500 B.C. In order to create this innovation, they had to be very skilled in working with metals as well as breeding and domesticating the proper oxen to pull the plows.

It might seem strange that the Egyptians would need this type of plow since they were living in the desert. However, the Nile River provided fertile black soil and this is where they plowed and planted their crops.

IRRIGATION

IRRIGATION

At certain times of the year, the Nile River flooded and at certain times the waters significantly decreased. The Egyptians used principles of hydraulic engineering to create specialized irrigation systems.

Archaeologists have uncovered evidence that they used these systems during the 12th dynasty. The systems were designed to provide water during times when there was drought. They used a lake to store their extra water for use when it was needed.

GLASS PERFUME BOTTLE

GLASS

The Ancient Egyptians had the ability to craft glass beads of varying colors. They began this work with glass around 1500 BC during the New Kingdom. These beads were highly sought after and the Egyptians traded them for other goods they needed.

They made the beads by taking a metal bar and winding liquid glass around it. Just as with many of their other types of art, the beads had a spiritual significance and were thought to have magical powers. In addition to beads they crafted glass bottles and jars.

FURNITURE

The Egyptians also crafted elaborate pieces of furniture. We know this because artifacts were found in some of the sealed-up tombs of the Pharaohs. There were beds, carved thrones, tables, chairs, and stools. Some of today's furniture has been modeled after their designs.

BED OF TUTANKHAMUN

ASTRONOMICAL CLOCK

ASTRONOMY

The Egyptians studied the night sky with precision and recorded their observations. Many of their religious beliefs as well as their scientific innovations were based on their studies of the skies.

They created circular walls out of bricks made with mud so they could mark the position of the sun as it rose. They made a record of the solstices, so they knew when the sun had reached its highest or lowest point in the sky at noon. They used plumb-bobs to make these measurements. They continued to refine their calendar based on their astronomical findings.

DENTAL HYGIENE

Another innovation by the Egyptians is the invention of toothpaste. They hadn't yet figured out how to remove the grit that was baked into their bread and they were having problems with their teeth. They invented the toothbrush and made the first toothpaste out of a variety of ingredients including eggshells, ox hooves that were ground up, and leftover ashes.

ANCIENT EGYPTIAN WOMAN
APPLYING MAKE UP

MAKEUP

The Egyptians invented makeup and both men and women wore it both as a fashion statement and to protect their skin from the desert sun. The dark kohl that they used around their eyes was a combination of soot and other minerals. This is the idea that started modern-day eyeliner.

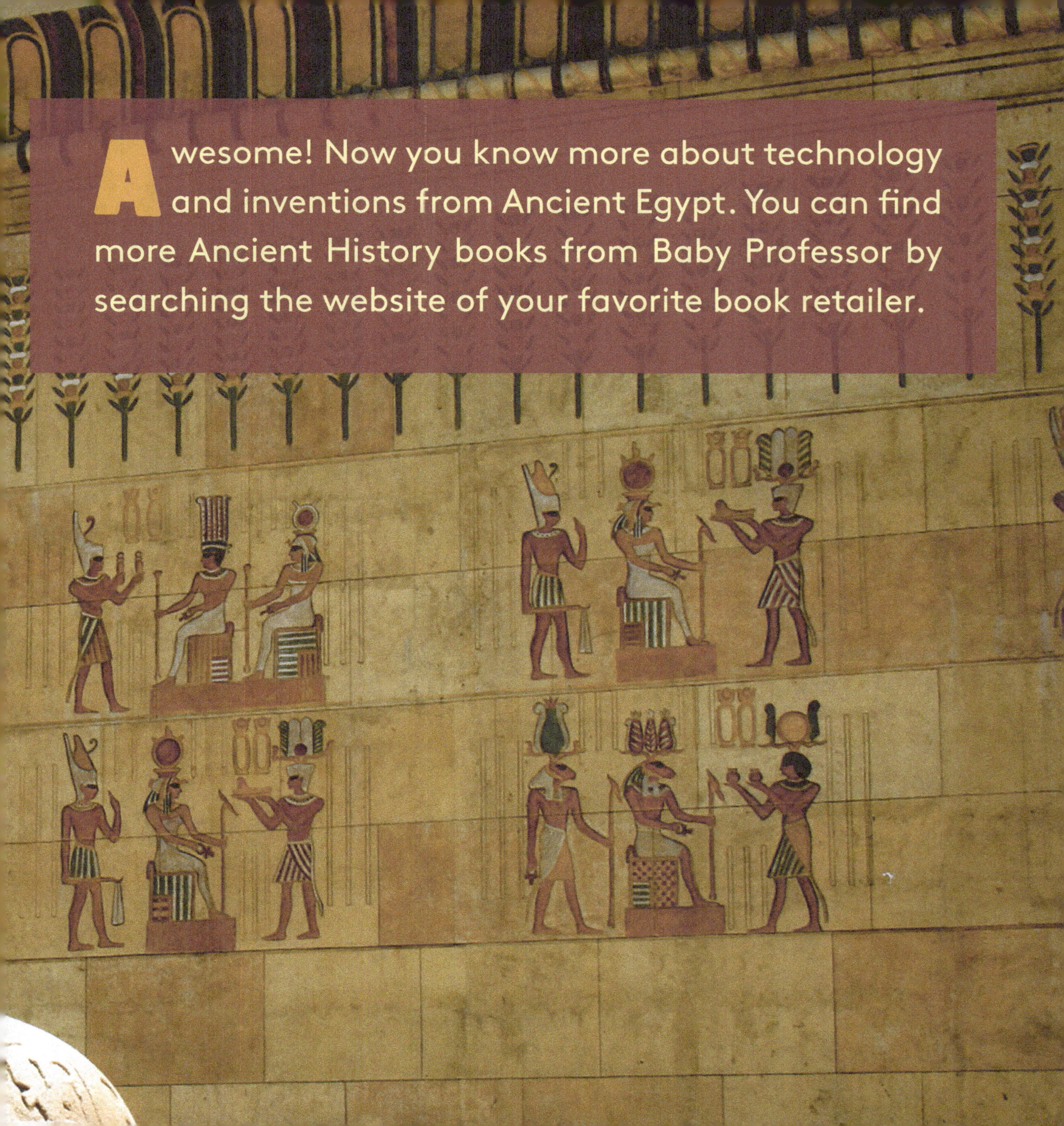

Awesome! Now you know more about technology and inventions from Ancient Egypt. You can find more Ancient History books from Baby Professor by searching the website of your favorite book retailer.

Visit
BABY PROFESSOR
EDUCATION KIDS
www.BabyProfessorBooks.com
to download Free Baby Professor eBooks
and view our catalog of new and exciting
Children's Books